MOON GARDEN

Also by Melody Godfred

Self Love Poetry: For Thinkers & Feelers

The ABCs of Self Love

The Shift: Poetry for a New Perspective

MOON GARDEN

poetry for manifestation

MELODY GODFRED

Andrews McMeel
PUBLISHING®

The authorised representative in the EEA is Simon and Schuster Netherlands BV, Herculesplein 96 3584 AA Utrecht, Netherlands. (info@simonandschuster.nl)

Andrews McMeel Publishing
a division of Andrews McMeel Universal
1130 Walnut Street, Kansas City, Missouri 64106

www.andrewsmcmeel.com

25 26 27 28 29 SDB 10 9 8 7 6 5 4 3 2 1

ISBN: 979-8-8816-0004-4

Library of Congress Control Number: 2025931873

Editor: Patty Rice
Art Director: Julie Barnes
Production Editor: Kelsey Rolofson
Production Manager: Julie Skalla

Illustrations by Dustin Kalynuk

FSC www.fsc.org MIX Paper | Supporting responsible forestry FSC® C144853

By the moon!

PROLOGUE

This story begins and ends with the scent of jasmine.

For many years now, if I pause on the step leading into my living room after the sun goes down, I'm greeted by the unmistakable scent of night-blooming jasmine. I've long called jasmine my olfactory ghost because it finds me even when none is planted nearby and no windows are open. In June of 2023, in the magical city of Ojai, California, my ghost was finally ready to explain her presence.

From the moment I arrived in Ojai, jasmine found me everywhere I went: on the walls of the Capri Hotel where I booked a last-minute room; in the first chapter of the used book I picked up at Bart's Books, the largest outdoor bookstore in the world ("The glorious scent of jasmine permeates the air"). The book, synchronistically, was written by my high school classmate's father about his wife, who visited him from the spirit world after passing. Jasmine tea found me again at Magic Hour, a local tea shop, where it was served to me by a lovely shop assistant. Her name? Also Jasmine. When I posted on social media about jasmine being my ghost, a stranger named Daisy shared the words that are now the foundation of the book you are holding in your hands: moon garden.

I now understand jasmine to be my intuition. This is the book my intuition wanted me to write.

INTRODUCTION

A moon garden is designed to be experienced by moonlight. It is filled with white and silver flowers that reflect moonshine and night-blooming plants that fill the air with their perfume. With a rich history that spans centuries, moon gardens have served as the ideal setting for everything from midnight trysts to moonlit meditations.

The moon garden invites you to leave the external world behind and explore an inner sanctuary where your true self is free to breathe, let go, explore, dance, and dream. While a typical garden is ruled by the sun, the moon garden reveres the moon.

According to The Old Farmer's Almanac *(and the Native American traditions from which much of the almanac derives), every year we are gifted twelve unique moons, each with its own name, energy, themes, and rituals. Moon by moon and poem by poem, this poetic manifestation book will nurture your journey of self-discovery and co-creation in alignment with the universe. As you embrace nature's rhythm, you will unlock your deepest desires, truths, and purpose. By honoring your intuition, setting intentions, and taking daily action, manifestation—the realization of your dreams—will naturally follow.*

It's important to note that our calendar is based on the solar rather than the lunar cycle, so the timing of new moons and full moons shifts each month. Some months may include two full moons or two new moons, while others may have none. Sometimes the new moon will appear first; other times, the full moon. The goal of Moon Garden *is not to offer a perfect science; instead, it seeks to gently inspire you to connect with the lunar cycle and, in turn, activate your own alchemy. In the same vein, although this book starts in January, according to lunar tradition, the new year doesn't begin until March. If January's "New year, new you!" messaging doesn't resonate with you, you're not alone. When we follow the moon's lead, we realize that January isn't the time to take action; it's the time to enter your inner world, express your truest self, and make space for your intuition's divine downloads—which is exactly what January's wolf moon is all about.*

In Moon Garden, *you'll experience the four seasons: new beginnings in spring, joyful expansion in summer, grateful completion in fall, and rest and contemplation in winter. For each moon, I offer an overarching theme, as well as suggestions for what to reclaim on the new moon and what to release on the full moon. These themes are designed to empower your unique rituals and manifestations for the year. I encourage you not only to read this book but also to explore other modalities like journaling, meditation, and movement to deepen your experience.*

Ultimately, you get to decide when to start this book and how to read it. Trust yourself. My hope is that as you read Moon Garden: Poetry for Manifestation, *you'll take yourself out to the garden, commune with the moon, and start manifesting the life you alone were born to live.*

MEET THE
MOONS

SPRING: NEW BEGINNINGS

CHOOSE

LOVE

BLOOM

SUMMER: JOYFUL EXPANSION

INDULGE

DARE

RESTORE

FALL: GRATEFUL COMPLETION

APPRECIATE

PUSH

COMPLETE

WINTER: REST AND CONTEMPLATION

REST

COMMUNE

SURRENDER

January Wolf Moon

COMMUNE

New Wolf Moon: Reclaim Vulnerability

Full Wolf Moon: Release Repression

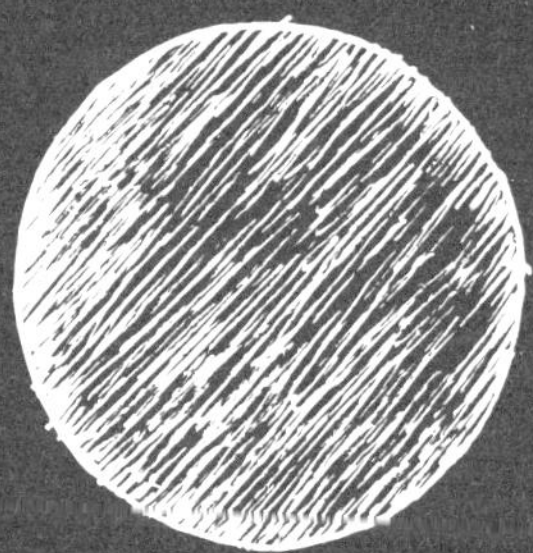

WOLF MOON

January moon. Wolf moon.
No more hiding moon.
Express your truth moon.
Take a breath, take a chance moon.
Your silence isn't serving you moon.
We don't have to do this alone moon.
I'll reveal me, you reveal you moon.
Commune with yourself moon.
Commune with me moon.
Let's be free moon.

JANUARY MANIFESTATION

Unleash your inner wild.
Be brave enough to howl.
What do you hunger for?
What have you been hiding?
Stop holding back.
Connect with your pack.
Give yourself permission.
Open your heart
Cast the spell: speak.

The foundation of manifesting our dreams is living authentically. It sounds so simple, so obvious, and yet we spend our lifetimes repressing our true selves. We lose touch with our intuition, with our desires. We fall silent. We abandon our unique purpose to maintain control and security. In the process, we end up designing lives we don't even want.

What if we collectively decide that instead of repressing ourselves, we will bravely be our messy, beautiful, singular selves. Imagine the impact: eight billion flowers suddenly blooming all at once.

MOON GARDEN

If I must have regrets,
let me have regrets.
The darkness will absolve me.
If I must fail,
let me fail.
The moon will console me.
If my heart must break,
let it break.
The garden will heal me.
Because I'd rather say
I lived, I really lived,
than be a seed that
never dared to bloom.

If your silence
is the only reason
it's working . . .
it's not working.

BREAKING GROUND

There is no more time for my silence.
Is who I am finally enough?
A million ways I've repressed
myself to meet your mold.
But if I appear broken, ask yourself:
did you accept all of me when I was whole?

In the garden, no one needs to convince the flower to let in the bee. The survival of each depends on it. They are not only bound by their mutuality, they are protected by it. Are we so different from the flower and the bee? If I am vulnerable with you, couldn't you be vulnerable with me? Maybe if we are more open, we can be more connected. Maybe we, too, can help each other survive.

SECRET GARDEN

If my vulnerability is a prayer,
your love is the answer.
I show you where I buried my seeds,
and you water my secrets until they bloom.

Resilience is no longer my ability to independently weather the storm and bounce back. Resilience is, instead, my willingness to be vulnerable and authentic, even when it is hard. Resilience is sharing what I am going through, letting people in, and receiving love and support, even though my self-preservation instinct tells me to go it alone. The wolf in me knows that my resilience depends not on me but on us. I am no lone wolf. I need my pack.

THE AWAKENING

For too long I was
unwilling to blossom.
Suffocating in my loneliness,
self-protection my only aim.
Until one night in the garden,
I realized we're so close
our petals can touch,
as long as I am willing to open.

A few months ago, my mom told me about a conflict she was experiencing where she felt like she couldn't express or honor her needs. We were having this conversation in our native tongue, which my six-year-old son, Teddy, can't understand. Despite that, when we finished, he went up to my mom and whispered in her ear: "Let me tell you a secret. It's your life. You can do what you want."

When you express your needs, the universe will find a way to provide the answer you are seeking. Listen to Teddy's advice and live your life.

MIDNIGHT CONFESSIONAL

My doubt?
I confess it to the moon.
She begs for it.
My heartache?
I confess it to the moon.
She is hungry for it.
My rage?
I confess it to the moon.
She burns for it.
I speak it all away until
all that's left in me is love.
That, the moon wants
me to keep.

Deep below your "I'm okay, it's okay" conditioning is your primal self, the version of you with a thirst for life, connection, pleasure, and play. The one who would never settle for "okay." That intuitive, daring force of nature is still within you—no matter how long it has been hibernating under the tundra of your daily routine.

Speak your truth. Let. YOU. Out.

S.O.S.

Once again,
my essence calls up
from the well of sacrifice
I've quietly dug myself into.
She howls:
I'm still here!
I'm still here!
I'm still here!
I remember my depth
and throw down a rope.
This time, I rescue myself.

WOLF MOON AFFIRMATION

With a heart full of gratitude and joy, I heed the wolf moon's call and commune with nature, with my community, and with myself. I reclaim vulnerability and release repression. I see vulnerability not as a weakness but as a portal. I keep my heart open. When I am open, the universe hears me. When I am open, I receive and reciprocate. It is safe for me to express myself. It is safe for me to be true. It is also safe for you. We no longer repress our essence. Together, we are free.

February Snow Moon

SURRENDER

New Snow Moon: Reclaim Stillness

Full Snow Moon: Release Control

SNOW MOON

February moon. Snow moon.
Clear the path by allowing it moon.
Be still and surrender moon.
Let this be enough moon.
Loosen your grip moon.
Nature's got this moon.
Maybe it can be this easy moon.
It's already in motion moon.
It already is moon.

FEBRUARY MANIFESTATION

Embrace the stillness.
Embody the pause.
What is waiting to bloom?
What is blooming?
What do you want?
Quiet your mind.
Open your heart.
Let your intuition guide you.
You have the answers.

*When your intuition
asks you questions,
what it's really doing is
leading you to the answers.
Be still. Listen.*

SOUL MAP

If the sunlit sky offers no guidance,
be like the songbirds who follow the stars.
Each constellation a love letter
to your intuition from the moon,
a map for migration
that leads your soul home.

Every winter, trees let go of their leaves to conserve energy as they prepare for new growth. Do they fear their own nakedness? No way. Trees do not stand in the way of their own manifestations.

How many of your old leaves are you clinging to while secretly wishing for something new? How exhausted you must be.

NEW WORLD ORDER

Instead of fearfully controlling,
I am joyfully receiving.
An unknown tomorrow,
a gift I give to myself.

Instead of desperately resisting,
I am gently relinquishing.
My conscious surrender
the birth of every new chapter.

Instead of silently withholding,
I am bravely revealing.
This bridge of truth
we walk on toward each other.

As someone who constantly thinks I've lost something, I'm learning that I only ever find it when I surrender it in my mind. My desire to do something about it, my anxiety about finding it, the overwhelming need to be in control at all times, that's what stands in the way of the discovery. Let it go. Let it come to you.

WHITE FLAG

Once I surrendered
my need for control,
I discovered my peace.
Once I surrendered
my expectations,
I discovered my curiosity.
Once I surrendered my regret,
I discovered my presence.
Once I surrendered
my need to know,
I discovered my knowing.

While snowdrop bulbs appear to lie dormant beneath the earth, they are actually quite busy preparing for spring. They first develop strong roots, growing down and anchoring themselves. They then gather water and nutrients, storing them for when it is time to reveal their delicate white blossoms. The cold itself signals to them that it is almost time, prompting the bulbs to start the metabolic processes required to push through the snow. By embracing their season of stillness, snowdrops lay the foundation for their own greatness.

Are we so different from the snowdrops?

ETERNAL SPRING

Hope revealed itself
just when I was about
to stop looking.
The only bud bursting
from a barren earth.
The one who believed
that even after the darkness,
life was still worth living.

If your ego asks,
"Is it my fault?
Did I do something wrong?"

Listen to your heart, which
gently suggests, "Is it your fault,
or are you trying to control
an undesirable outcome
by blaming yourself?"

SPIRALING

The spirals in nature,
shells, moonflowers, even galaxies,
are all welcome signs of evolution.

Except the spirals in my mind,
these I judge, I reject
as unwelcome
signs of my demise.

But maybe, with each spiral,
I, too, am evolving,
even ascending,
as each spiral unravels
who I am not,
so I can rise up
to who I am.

The Japanese concept of seijaku *defines stillness not as a passive retreat but as active calm amidst the hustle of daily life. It invites the tranquility, peace, and quiet of a Zen garden into one's daily life. It sees stillness not as an absence but rather as a presence.*

Can you be powerfully still?
What will you discover?
What will you receive?
What will you offer?

SILENT SYMPHONY

In the moon garden,
the song of time slows,
her steady march replaced
by a symphony of stillness.
Only in silence did I finally hear
the sound of my dreams awakening,
a new key of life playing its very first notes

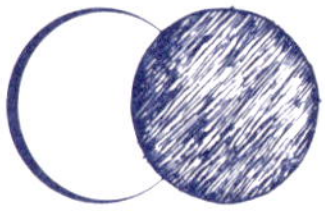

SNOW MOON AFFIRMATION

With a heart full of gratitude and joy, I embody the snow moon and surrender. I reclaim stillness and release control. I give up my need for knowing everything and my insatiable desire to do more. I honor my intrinsic right to be still. To trust. To receive. To play telephone with the universe, my intuition the string between our windows. I welcome not being in charge or in a rush. I finally stop blaming myself. I have the answers because I am the answer. I push through the snow. I am ready.

March Worm Moon

CHOOSE

New Worm Moon:
Reclaim Metamorphosis

Full Worm Moon: Release Resistance

WORM MOON

March moon. Worm moon.
Dreams set in motion moon.
Show, don't tell moon.
Awaken the earth moon.
Plant the seeds moon.
Build momentum moon.
Visualize the sweetness moon.
Choose and transform moon.
Your spring is here moon.

MARCH MANIFESTATION

Feel the gentle stirring.
Awaken from hibernation.
What is calling you?
What is holding you back?
Keep clearing space.
Trust your knowing.
Commit to your plans.
Inch by inch,
make a choice and begin.

A seed for even the most extraordinary flower is just an unassuming seed until it is planted. The same is true for your ideas. Take the first step and plant the seed. Instead of waiting for inspiration, draw, write, play, dance, express yourself however you can. Set into motion your own metamorphosis. The world needs your soul's one-of-a-kind expression now more than ever.

THE ART OF DOING SOMETHING

Writing the poem.
Dancing the dance.
Sharing the song.
Practicing the ritual.
Finding the time.
Crafting the plan.
Planting the garden.
Breaking the pattern.
Taking the risk.
Embracing the change.
Making the choice.

Go to the garden and
choose a flower to admire.
Take in her singular beauty.
Now you know: making choices
is only hard when you think
there is a wrong one.

QUIET REVOLUTION

Change is not a new season,
a date on a calendar,
a solstice celebration.
Change is moment to moment,
choice by choice,
bloom by bloom.
The conviction that takes
what has always been and
quietly makes it something new.

Imagine it is fall. You claw back the dirt with your bare hands and lay down bulbs for poet's narcissus: white-petaled daffodils. Then, throughout the winter, you surrender. You allow. You anticipate but never hurry. You let the invisible work happen while you rest. Until finally, one humble day in March, emergence. Shoots, green and strong, come through the earth. Over the next month, the daffodil reveals herself, bit by bit. Her buds swell as she prepares to announce her blooms. She knows this is her season, just as you know it is yours. The spring in each of you is the same. Soon, she will be wearing her crown, and so will you: a shared reward for taking your time and gently embracing what each season has to offer.

MY METAMORPHOSIS

I watch the leaves
sacrifice themselves
at the altar of fall.
Branches lay themselves
bare each winter.
Buds cast themselves
open in spring, and
birds ground themselves
to nest for summer.
When change is so abundant
all around me,
how silly of me to think
it is my right to stay the same.

Discover your points of resistance and move toward them with infinite curiosity. Your manifestation isn't hidden in your instant yeses; it is waiting for you in your most visceral nos.

MEET THE MOMENT

When today challenges me,
I will meet the moment.
When today delights me,
I will meet the moment.
Without resistance,
without attachment,
I become by being.
I will not run.

Regardless of her phase, the moon remains committed to her path across the sky. Imagine if the crescent moon refused to rise because she was not yet full. The moon knows no such resistance. Whatever stage you are at in your manifestation, be like the moon . . . and steadily ascend.

TENDER TRANSFORMATION

Just as the moon relieves the sun,
twilight romances the day,
silence softens the sounds,
stars adorn the sky, and
slowness unwinds time,
transformation is my birthright.
As long as I stop resisting
what nature wants for me,
as long as I lovingly embrace
my own becoming.

Metamorphosis can be painful and slow. In making your way to what you deeply desire, you have to give up the old way, the familiar comforts, the habits, the known. You must deliberately step into a future beyond the realities you've experienced, into a new realm beyond your perfect control. Like the hummingbird moth who pollinates in the darkness, you must simply trust your calling and bravely emerge.

ONWARD

And despite the world's many perils,
never once did the butterfly
try to return to the safety of its cocoon.

WORM MOON AFFIRMATION

With a heart full of gratitude and joy, I harness the worm moon's momentum and choose. I reclaim metamorphosis and release resistance. I commit to my intentions because I am no longer stifled by indecision, fear, or self-judgment. The path ahead is cleared by the choices I am now willing to make. I am making my way, in my own way and in my own time. I am evolving in co-creation with nature and in union with my process. I am the seed and the gardener. Together we grow.

April Pink Moon

LOVE

New Pink Moon: Reclaim Self Love

Full Pink Moon: Release Limitations

PINK MOON

April moon. Pink moon.
Behold the freedom of authenticity moon.
Shed what isn't in alignment moon.
Lay down the old stories moon.
Embark upon your soul path moon.
See yourself well moon.
Receive love and give love moon.
Be love moon.
Love moon.

APRIL MANIFESTATION

Liberate your authentic self.
Spring forth as your divine expression.
Can you abandon your limitations?
Can you engage your possibilities?
Align your life with your intentions.
Embrace your calling.
Vibrate higher and higher.
Are you ready to break through?
Are you ready to love?

You weren't born to please them.
You were born to be you.

BIRTHRIGHT

I was not born to be sorry,
smaller, full of shame,
or always in a rush.
I was not born to fit
in clothes, in your story,
in the narrow corridor
this culture carved for me.
I was not born to acquiesce,
to accommodate, or to appease.
To be less when I am so much more.
I was not born to earn
respect, money, status, or fame.
Always pushing myself
when we both know
it will never be enough.
I was born to be wildly myself.
To unfurl my soul at my pace.
To explore my gifts as I wish.
To take pleasure in presence.
To make time my servant,
the universe my accomplice,
this life my masterpiece.

Lately, every message the universe sends me is a message of love. She leaves me hearts everywhere I look: at the bottom of my coffee cup, in the concrete beneath my feet, in the drop of pancake batter that falls during the rush of our morning routine.

The hearts tell me what I think I've always known deep in my own heart: love is why we are here. Love is why we ARE. Our deepest purpose is to love ourselves, and from there, to love each other.

The hearts help me remember that love is the why of our existence. Love is the whole point.

SELF LOVE SEASON

Self love aligned me so that
my worth eclipsed my shame
my faith eclipsed my fear
my essence eclipsed my ego
my hope eclipsed my regret
my future eclipsed my past
my gratitude eclipsed my guilt
my peace eclipsed my pain
my possibilities eclipsed my limitations.

*Maybe adulthood is simply learning
to apologize for myself less and less
until there is nothing left to apologize
for and all that's left is love.*

BIRTHDAY WISH

I revisit every line of my life,
like every year before, but
this time with tender reflection
instead of painful rumination.
I curl myself around every memory
to shelter the flame
of my one and only essence.
The wish I make
is to love myself,
next year, even more.

Think of your intuition as night-blooming jasmine, the lady of the night. She emerges when it is quiet, when you are still. In the sacred darkness, she blooms to lead you home to yourself. Her star-shaped flowers offer divine guidance, a floral constellation for you to follow. She wraps herself around you, her sweet scent removing every possible barrier you have put up against love. She disarms you. In her presence, you have no choice but to return to your purest form. To love and be loved. To love yourself. That is what your intuition wants for you. Remember that when you smell her.

MY MIRROR

The love I crave
is a mirror that says
I see you fully
and I like what I see.
I am the mirror:
the love I crave
is my own.

My brother Jonny recently shared this with me.

"I used to see myself as either worse than or better than everyone around me. I now see myself as the same as.

"I used to see myself as separate from everyone around me. I now see myself as inherently connected to.

"It's the difference between being a unique individual and being a unique piece of a greater whole."

What else but love could remove so many barriers?

SELF CEREMONY

I choose myself
to have and to hold
in sickness and in health
in wholeness and in heartbreak
in clarity and in uncertainty
in joy and in despair
in steps forward and back
in solitude and in community
in moments sacred and mundane
with endless and ever-expanding love
in this world and the next, forevermore.

As soon as my daughter Stella learned to speak, she told me that she came from a place called the Love Moon. There, Stella slept on a bed of flowers, and her days were filled with song and dance.

She taught me that on the Love Moon, God is a woman, and Her only mandate is loving kindness. On the Love Moon, we are born to love, we are born to be kind, we are born to care for ourselves and each other.

The more I learn, the more I grow, and the more I heal, the more I believe we can all return to the Love Moon at any time. Will you come with me?

THE ANSWER IS YOUR LOVE

The thing that's missing?
The answer is your love.
The uncertainty that's bursting?
The answer is your love.
The fear that's crippling?
The answer is your love.
The loneliness that's crushing?
The answer is your love.
The decision that's looming?
The answer is your love.
The wound that isn't healing?
The answer is your love.
The dream that needs tending?
The answer is your love.

PINK MOON AFFIRMATION

With a heart full of gratitude and joy, I honor the pink moon's quest for love and commit fully to loving. I reclaim self love and release limitations. I no longer stand in my own way. I build a life that is in alignment with my authentic self. I tune in to my intuition for divine guidance and trust that I know best what is right for me. Love is my North Star and joyfully connects me to everyone and everything. When I love myself, I am limitless.

May Flower Moon

BLOOM

New Flower Moon: Reclaim Expansion

Full Flower Moon: Release Isolation

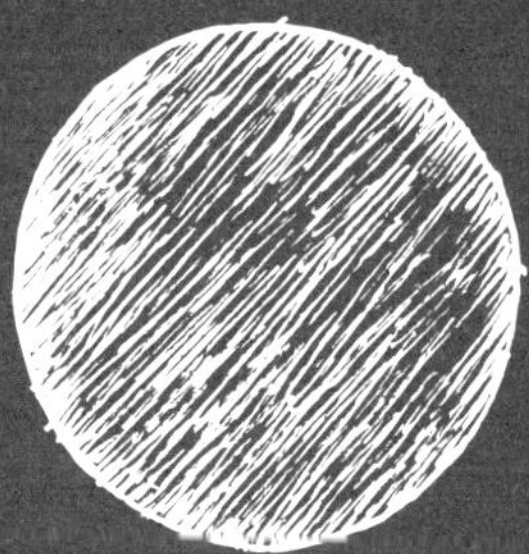

FLOWER MOON

May moon. Flower moon.
The quiet time is over moon.
Wonder and wander moon.
Get lost in your essence moon.
Explore the fertile grounds moon.
Expand beyond your borders moon.
The risk holds the reward moon.
Let's bloom together moon.

MAY MANIFESTATION

Engage with the world.
Grow in every direction.
Can you untether yourself completely?
Will you allow yourself even more?
Flourish into your wildest dreams.
Accept the invitations.
Enjoy the lushness.
Life is teeming.
Join in.

I thought being alone
would keep me safe.
In the end, all it did
was keep me alone.

BELTANE

On the first of May,
we taste summer
and feast on life's bloom.
Meet me at the bonfire.
For mother moon,
let's circle and sing.
In this sacred garden,
let's weave together
the ribbons of our lives.

Everyone focuses on the progress they can see. Moving forward, moving upward. But what about the expansion below the surface? How far down have your roots traveled? How many layers have you unraveled within yourself? Just how close have you come to your deepest truth? To your inner god? We focus so much on ascension. What I'm interested in is your depth.

THE INVITATION

Do you dare tread across
your own vastness?
To feel your possibility
in every direction?
To breathe in your own air,
to be your own water?
To be the one who feeds
the thirst of your being?

As a realist, I'm wired to be in a constant state of fight-or-flight. Every moment, a question. Am I safe? Am I safe? Am I safe? Vigilance is how I keep one foot on the brakes at all times, just in case. Dreaming always feels dangerous and entirely too vulnerable because what if I take a risk and everything falls apart? What if I let you in and you let me down? The truth is, the only thing my vigilance has ever accomplished is keeping me small, not safe. I'm ready for more—aren't you? Maybe the only safety we can offer each other is taking the risk and dreaming our dreams—together.

So I ask: what does the future look like if
everything works out exactly as we want it to?
Now what would happen if we
dreamed ten times bigger?

MY WISH FOR YOU (II)

To manifest without tension
to amplify without restriction
to transform without opposition
to indulge without inhibition
to dare without limitation
to dream without interruption
to love without hesitation
to heal without complication
to rejoice without disruption
to wildly be you without apology,
disclaimer, or condition.

Wildflowers are known as pioneer plants. That means they can survive in places other plants cannot, like a barren field or cracked concrete. As wildflowers take root, they create a better future for themselves, and for all other plants, too. From their ability to self-pollinate and heal the soil to their ample seeds and modest requirements for growth, everything about wildflowers is designed to beat the odds. Where others might have given up, wildflowers can help birth an ecosystem. Remember, you, too, are a pioneer, wild one . . . and there is a superbloom in your near future.

I AM THE ZODIAC

Every day, I embody
the courage of Aries,
the loyalty of Taurus,
the curiosity of Gemini,
the empathy of Cancer,
the confidence of Leo,
the order of Virgo,
the balance of Libra,
the passion of Scorpio,
the spontaneity of Sagittarius,
the perseverance of Capricorn,
the innovation of Aquarius,
the intuition of Pisces.
I am the zodiac in its entirety,
the cosmic promise,
the dreamer and the dream.

Did you know that bees dance to communicate good news to each other? When scout bees find a flower bursting with nectar, they race back to the hive and share the news by dancing. How they dance reveals what they've found and where it is located. Bees dance to share their wealth. Bees dance to share their joy.

When's the last time you danced for someone?
When's the last time you danced?

GROUNDING

Barefoot in the garden,
I realize I'm not so alone
in this life after all.
As a million blades of grass
tickle me forward,
they remind me
to laugh while I bloom.

All my life, I've feared wild mushrooms. So many warnings about their poison, their destructiveness in the garden. But recently I've learned about mycelium, the intricate network that lives below the surface and supports the mushrooms we see and the broader ecosystem around them. Mycelium plays a vital role in decomposing organic material and creating stable soil. It also forms symbiotic relationships with plants, enhancing their ability to absorb water and nutrients and even to communicate with each other.

Each time I shuddered at the sight of mushrooms in my garden, what I was really witnessing was the manifestation of life sustaining life beneath the soil. The mushroom is the flower of my garden's communal labor; it is the visible expression of how much becomes possible when we honor just how interconnected we all are.

THE DOOR IS OPEN

There is an endless sky
above our heads.
There is endless earth
beneath our feet.
As above, so below.
As within, so without.
In every moment
we stand together at the
threshold of infinity.
Walk with me.

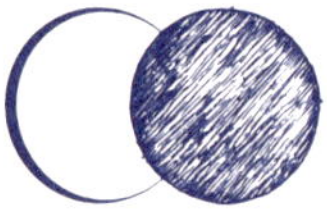

FLOWER MOON AFFIRMATION

With a heart full of gratitude and joy, I bask in the glow of the flower moon, and I bloom. I reclaim expansion and release isolation. I leave the confines of my solitude and am energized by human connection. I am in awe of my soul's expansiveness and amplify myself effortlessly. I grow up and forward but also deeper within myself. I have unlocked a future filled with infinite possibility and a present where I am safe to become my fullest expression. I am and have everything I need.

June Strawberry Moon

INDULGE

New Strawberry Moon: Reclaim Pleasure

Full Strawberry Moon: Release Perfection

STRAWBERRY MOON

June moon. Strawberry moon.
See the good moon.
Life is ripe moon.
Go a little slower moon.
Explore your joy moon.
Presence over perfection moon.
Know your pleasure moon.
Be here in your body moon.
To be alive is the gift moon.

JUNE MANIFESTATION

Honor your life force.
Practice your pleasure.
When are you most alive?
Can you indulge without apology?
Claim your desire.
Do away with perfection.
Enjoy the experiment.
Now is all we have.
This is your time.

I used to say "progress over perfection." Now I say "pleasure over perfection." Instead of making progress, I'm experiencing pleasure. Now. Instead of being stuck in a state of perpetual productivity, I'm going outside, putting on some music, having a cool drink, and dancing with the wildflowers. Because pleasure doesn't wait for us. It's not something you earn or work toward. It is utterly urgent. It can only be experienced here, today, right now. The wildflowers await. Won't you join me?

PHOENIX RISING

I transcend my hunger
for tomorrow's perfection
by being here—now.
I feed my heart on peace,
my soul on pleasure.
Because I am willing to fail,
I am free to begin—
again and again.
Eternally renewed,
continually ablaze.
Every dawn, I am reborn.

I was passing by someone in an aisle at the store and instinctively said, "I'm sorry."

He looked me dead in the eye and said, "You weren't put on this earth to be sorry. Be wild instead."

That's my advice for you, too.

REWILDING

Pleasure will return us.
A salve for technology addiction,
social isolation, and hips stiff
from sitting when all
we did before was dance.
Pleasure will return us.
Our liberation from fear,
judgment, anger, and separation.
Pleasure will return us.
To the place from which we came.
To the place where we belong.
To the garden. To the birds.
To each other.

I've come to realize the sky embodies every emotion. Anticipation is a sunrise. Joy is a clear, sunny day. Fear is a stormy midnight. Anger can be found in a burning sunset. Melancholy is twilight. Golden hour, love.

To see pleasure, look for the northern lights: flashes of color that erupt across a sleeping sky. They reflect not just an emotion but the very pulse of life itself.

Don't let your pleasure be as rare.

SUMMER UPGRADES

Pleasure over perfection.
Delight over disappointment.
Curiosity over certainty.
Tenderness over tough love.
Gratitude over guilt.
Balance over burnout.
Moments over milestones.
Connection over conflict.
Empathy over ego.
Healing over hustling.
Joy over jealousy.
Ease over excess.
Love over everything.

If you trace back the linguistic origin of "rose," you'll find yourself traveling through ancient Roman, Greek, and ultimately Persian history. "Rose" is thought to be derived from the Old Persian root *vrda-, which, when traced even farther back, takes us to its Proto-Indo-European root word, *wrdho-, which means "thorn."

The most popular flower in the world, the one most associated with love, passion, and beauty, is named not after its perfection but after its perceived pain point.

Perhaps our own power lies in embracing our imperfections, too.

ROSE MANDALA

Every rose has a thorn, and
every thorn has a rose.
If I am to bloom beyond
the bud of my being,
my pain and my pleasure
must learn to coexist.

Sometimes making yourself happy
will make someone else upset.
Resist the urge to doubt your desire.

PLEASURE PRINCIPLE

You misunderstand me
like you misunderstand the bee.

You think I'm here to sting you,
but all I'm looking to do
is make some honey.

Chasing perfection is like searching for a four-leaf clover. Experiencing pleasure is lying down in a field of clovers on the first day of summer.

Which will you choose?

PLEASURE IS NOT A LUXURY

A six-second hug.
The first sip of coffee.
Jeans that fit just right.
Deep belly laughs.
Fresh flowers in your kitchen.
Getting lost in a bookstore.
Your bed after a long day.
Digging your hands into the dirt.
A walk with a friend.
The sun on your bare skin
The electric feel of live music.
Dancing in the moonlight.
Deliberate inhales and exhales.
Reading poetry.
This very moment.

STRAWBERRY MOON AFFIRMATION

With a heart full of gratitude and joy, I taste the sweetness of the strawberry moon and allow myself to indulge. I reclaim pleasure and release perfection. I see the present moment for what it is: an opportunity to explore, for joy. I abandon my need for achievement, perfection, and lucky outcomes, and instead embrace the power of simply being myself, here and now. I smell the roses. I eat the berries. I remember I am here to be alive.

July Buck Moon

DARE

New Buck Moon: Reclaim Trust

Full Buck Moon: Release Fear

BUCK MOON

July moon. Buck moon.
Feel your vitality moon.
Honor your own rhythm moon.
Transmute your fear moon.
The unknown is your ally moon.
Be a little braver moon.
Set your sights on it moon.
Your desire is attainable moon.
Dare to have it moon.

JULY MANIFESTATION

Go ahead and trust.
Step fully into the dream.
What are you afraid of?
Can you learn to love it?
Release your anchors.
Shed your inhibitions.
Claim your destiny.
Run toward it.
It's yours.

Fear is when you look over your shoulder.
Trust is when you look up at the moon.
Where will you rest your gaze?

ETERNAL OPTIMIST

What are you looking for?
they asked.

The moon,
I said.

Always the moon.

If you've ever watched a time-lapse video of a Midnight Moon dahlia, you'll notice an interesting phenomenon: its petals seem to contract before bursting open. One might think this is an act of fear or uncertainty, a retreat inward before the ultimate act of vulnerability: blooming. In reality, dahlias turn inward to gather energy, read the environment, and realign each lavender-edged petal to achieve its fullest expression. Like us, dahlias follow circadian rhythms that guide them through cycles of rest and growth. They dare to bloom, yes, but they do so in their own time and in their own way.

THE ORACLE

I hold space for myself, and time stands still.
I feel eternity cycling between my hands.
Oh, the power of releasing myself
from my ever-worried mind.
In this pause, my essence reveals herself.
I ask how we will find our way forward.
In my own voice, she lovingly says,
"Trust yourself."

You can welcome it with love
or dismiss it with fear.
Either way, tomorrow comes.
I choose love.

BIRDSONG

I heard once
that listening to birdsong
calms the body
because birds only sing
when predators aren't near.
I hope this is true.
I will listen to the birds
even if it is not.

During the daytime, while a moonflower is still a closed bud, no one can fathom her nocturnal splendor. To achieve the magnitude of her true self, the moonflower must trust the darkness all around her. As the moon rises and the moonflower spirals open, she grows three times in size to reveal a star-shaped center. Even though she only flowers for a single night, the moonflower doesn't fear what lies on the other side of her becoming. She simply trusts herself to bloom.

Will you forever remain a tight bud, or are you ready to see what happens when you embrace the darkness, too?

ANGELS PLAY HERE

If I am meant to fear the darkness,
tell me why the nightingales sing,
moonflowers bloom,
and fireflies dance
across dew-kissed fields.

Tell me why moonlight
makes the oceans glitter,
why stars shine brighter
the darker it becomes.

If I am meant to fear the darkness,
tell me why angels love to linger here,
the shadows we avoid
their favorite playground.

If darkness is not a gift,
tell me why it illuminates so much,
this sanctuary where the wild dreams are.

The moon in me is rising.
She reminds me to be brave.

PANDORA'S BOX

When I dared to open
the box of unknowns,
I realized the perils
I feared were already here.
Inside the future,
only hope awaited me.

In the garden I ask myself four questions:

What if it will be okay?
What if there is enough?
What if it doesn't matter?
What if not knowing is the only way?

PLAN B(LOOM)

Mary asked me what my plan is
for this one wild and precious life.

My plan is simple:
I'm planting thousands of wildflowers
and joyfully waiting to see what happens.

BUCK MOON AFFIRMATION

With a heart full of gratitude and joy, I am emboldened by the buck moon, and so I dare. I reclaim trust and release fear. I realize that the unknown used to keep me where I was; now, the unknown pulls me toward where I need to be. Fear is no longer the barrier; fear is now the invitation. I trust myself; I trust the universe. Whatever the future holds in store for me, I am brave enough to bloom my way to it. The moon in me leads the way.

August Sturgeon Moon

RESTORE

New Sturgeon Moon: Reclaim Wholeness

Full Sturgeon Moon: Release Shame

STURGEON MOON

August moon. Sturgeon moon.
Let the past be your medicine moon.
Lift the veil of shame moon.
You deserve to be seen moon.
No part of you left behind moon.
Your wholeness is holy moon.
Love your inner monster moon.
Restore your fullest self moon.
Your future requires all of you moon.

AUGUST MANIFESTATION

Stir past the surface.
Dive into your shadow.
Can you embrace your wrongness?
Can you reframe your shame?
Integrate your many selves.
Heal the broken narrative.
Abandon the limiting beliefs.
Activate your total power.
Your dream future awaits.

Despite their common classification as weeds, dandelions are one of the most valuable plants you can have in the garden. From providing pollen to bees when other plants are scarce, to aerating the soil, to being edible from blossom to root, dandelions are hardly the nuisance they're made out to be. In fact, they are adaptable, resilient, and grow rapidly and plentifully. They are medicine, not just for the soil but for us. Why, then, are they considered weeds? Because they are adaptable, resilient, and inclined to grow.

Our superpowers are often inextricably linked with our vulnerabilities, especially when we let other people's judgments define our worth.

Dandelions are always welcome in the moon garden. So are you.

DANDELION

When I was young and golden,
you called me a weed, but
what I am is the flower of life.
The sun, moon, and stars at once.
Instead of dying, I grant wishes.
With each hopeful breath,
I am reborn a thousand times,
a firework exploding for eternity.

My self love journey has allowed me to recover the parts of myself I once abandoned to please others. With each piece of myself that I reintegrate, the memories of the people who didn't see or appreciate the true me start to fade. My wholeness is what heals my heartbreak: it allows me to release them and reclaim me.

THE DAISY GAME

I pick myself apart:
he loves me,
he loves me not.
In trying to please
you instead of me,
I sacrifice what
once made me whole.
I sacrifice what once
made you want me.

In my family, when we make a wish, it's always followed with, "By the moon!" It isn't rare to find my mom outside at night with her hands stretched up to the moon in prayer. No one taught her to do this, but as women, our connection to the moon is primal.

Each month, the moon unapologetically cycles across the sky, yet we shamefully ignore or repress our own cyclical nature. The moon is my reminder to recognize and express myself fully, in all my phases.

MATRIARCHY

My grandmother's moon
is my mother's moon
is my moon.
She is what connects
our prayers
to each other.

I am not a human body
born into the cosmos.

I am the cosmos
born into a human body.

MIRACLE IS MY NAME

My past, present,
and future selves
together form a family.
They hold me tight
and lovingly say:
the greatest miracle
of this life will
always be you.

If there is sadness to be felt,
it is your responsibility to feel it.
Without the rain, there can be no garden.

THE MERMAID

Each full moon,
I let the tides pull me
into the healing blue.
Because only there,
under Luna's glow,
do I remember:
my salt is as welcome
as my sweetness.

Gardenia and tuberose are thought to release past trauma and facilitate emotional healing and balance by enhancing clarity and calm. Create a small altar under the full moon with candles, fresh gardenias, and tuberoses (or use essential oils), and write about your deepest memories of shame. At the end of each reflection, smell the flowers and envision meeting your shame with love, kindness, and acceptance. Every time you smell these healing floral scents, let them be a reminder that you are always worthy of unconditional love.

CELESTIAL BODY

I trace my fingers
across my skin and
remember that, like constellations,
my body is worthy of being mapped,
witnessed, and wondered about
with awe, for generations.

STURGEON MOON AFFIRMATION

With a heart full of gratitude and joy, I follow the sturgeon moon, and I restore myself. I reclaim my wholeness and release my shame. I am empowered by my story instead of encumbered by it. I know my darkness and revel in it, just as I do my light. I play with my shadow and integrate all aspects of myself. I stand confidently at the lion's gate and walk toward forever as my fullest self. No part of me is off-limits. All of me deserves all my love.

September Harvest Moon

APPRECIATE

New Harvest Moon: Reclaim Abundance

Full Harvest Moon: Release Disappointment

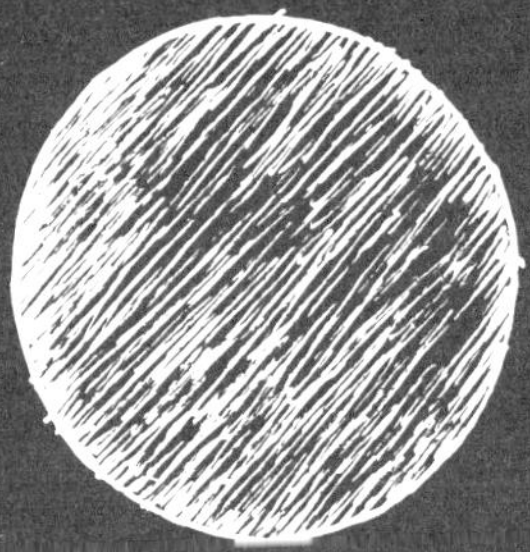

HARVEST MOON

September moon. Harvest moon.
Witness your progress moon.
Pause and bask in it moon.
Reap the abundance moon.
Let gratitude envelop you moon.
Step back and slow down moon.
Restore your balance moon.
See what is now moon.
Appreciate all of it moon.

SEPTEMBER MANIFESTATION

Root into the moment.
Take stock of your labors.
What's ready for harvest?
What more must be done?
Relish the richness.
Be present enough to have it.
Let go of your disappointment.
Lovingly receive all that there is.
You worked hard for this.

While March's worm moon brought us the spring equinox, and with it a period of emergence, action, and momentum, September's autumnal equinox under the harvest moon offers us a pause for reflection, gratitude, and presence. In many ways, they are mirror opposites that ground each other.

Now is the time to witness the abundance you've cultivated throughout this year. See it. Be in it. Harvest it. Then ask yourself: by the first of December, how do I want to feel? This feeling will be your road map for the next two moons.

MOONSHOT

When I look back
on my life,
all I wish to say is,
"I regret nothing."
That is enough for me.

Gratitude is the gateway to abundance and the antidote to disappointment. When you notice what's there instead of what's missing, what you already have immediately blooms.

A QUANTUM OF JOY

My reality is responsive.
Noticing shifts my timeline.
What I observe, I become.
What I am, I see.
When joy is the witness,
joy is what's witnessed.

If no one notices that it's harvest time, the fruit is left to rot. Don't forget to harvest the fruits of your labor.

PROMISED LAND

Abundance doesn't seek emptiness.
It isn't interested in filling a black hole,
sand poured into an endless abyss.
Abundance seeks fullness.
A fertile ground to grow upon.
A gardener intent upon
enjoying her garden.
Someone who sees the flowers
she worked so hard to grow.

The word present, *meaning "the now," and the word* present, *"a gift," share a linguistic origin that explains why these two seemingly unrelated concepts rely on the same word. They derive from the same Latin root,* prae-, *becoming both "immediate" and "to place in front of": in other words, to make an offering, now.*

When you give someone a gift, you're making an offering to them. Time, too, is making an offering to us, in every present moment. Will you receive it?

A PRESENT FOR YOU

If you can believe
that maybe tomorrow
everything can change . . .

maybe you can also believe
that today, even right now,
everything can change, too.

If you allow it.

Things we've been chasing:
our potential, external validation,
tomorrow's elusive promises.

Things available to us when we slow down:
our worth, internal validation,
today's many gifts.

MOONCHILD

Who am I but a girl
with flowers in her hair,
moonlight in her eyes,
and a deep knowing that
regardless of her season,
no matter her phase,
she is always enough.

The harvest moon reminds us that balance is the natural order. The sun must set, the moon must rise, and in late September, day and night achieve near-perfect equilibrium.

The same is true for our relationships. We cannot exclusively give and then be surprised by the disharmony that follows. Like the sun and the moon, we must rise, and we must rest. We must give abundantly, yes, but we must also be willing to receive . . . abundantly.

TENDERNESS

The gardener thinks
she is tending to the garden.
The garden thinks
it is tending to her.
Neither challenges the other.
Both are simply tended to

HARVEST MOON AFFIRMATION

With a heart full of gratitude and joy, I am inspired by the harvest moon and am ready to appreciate. I reclaim abundance and release disappointment. I recognize how far I have come and trust myself to complete the rest of my journey. I allow myself to be present enough to enjoy what is and to flow through my life with balance, peace, and ease. I shift effortlessly between giver and receiver as I notice and celebrate the bounty all around me.

October Hunter Moon

PUSH

New Hunter Moon: Reclaim Devotion

Full Hunter Moon: Release Doubt

HUNTER MOON

October moon. Hunter moon.
Hard work is welcome moon.
You've got this moon.
Push through and complete it moon.
No challenge too great moon.
Let your ancestors fortify you moon.
Affirm the new pattern moon.
Prepare for fulfillment moon.
Inner warrior moon.

OCTOBER MANIFESTATION

Commit to your manifestations.
Only you can see them through.
How devoted are you willing to be?
Can you renounce every doubt?
Be certain about your intentions.
Rise above any resistance.
Pull from your well of power.
Align with your highest vision.
You're closer than you think.

It's natural to reach a roadblock and think, "This is a sign I should stop." But imagine, instead, that this very struggle is designed to unlock something that's already within you: something deeper, more powerful, more essential.

What if hardship is the portal to manifestation?

What if the hard part is the key?

THE REMEDY

Where there is doubt, meet it with love.
Where there is doubt, meet it with curiosity.
Where there is doubt, meet it with devotion.
Where there is doubt, meet it with service.
Where there is doubt, meet it with,
"There is a reason I am here;
there is something for me to discover;
there is more room for me to grow."

If you're only hanging on by a thread,
it means you've already unraveled.
The hardest part is behind you.
Now is not the time to stop.

SPIDER WOMAN

My web of resilience
remained hidden
until the rain came
and adorned me
with liquid diamonds.
Where once I was covered
in the dust of doubt,
now I wear
a lattice of crystal lace.
I used to look to you
for protection.
Now, breath by breath,
I weave my own sanctuary.

It is easy to think that our inability to manifest stems from a failure of vision; that until we understand our purpose with perfect clarity, we remain stuck between who we are and who we want to be. But the truth is far less transcendent. The secret is not grand visions but daily commitments. The magic is trapped in the mundane.

Manifestation depends on our willingness to align our actions with our intentions, moment to moment, choice by choice. There is no such thing as an instant transformation. The caterpillar breaks itself down to nothing before pushing itself back out into the world, this time reborn with wings.

How far beyond your doubt are you willing to venture? How devoted are you willing to be?

THE DEEP END

Toe the shores of your desires.
Feel the chill and go deeper anyway.
Be enveloped by your devotion.
Go deeper still.
With each crashing wave,
experience a wet world.
A world where
it's allowed to be easy,
to know what you want,
and to have it.

Always remember: expectations never made a flower bloom any faster. Whatever stage you are in, receive yourself with care and patience. Sometimes you'll move fast; sometimes slow. Sometimes you'll do more; sometimes less. You are valid regardless of your speed or productivity. Go easy on yourself, but keep going. You deserve to see this through.

LATE BLOOMER

You say I'm too late.
I missed the milestones.
I failed life's tests.
But I say
I'm an aster,
a chrysanthemum,
a Japanese anemone.
I bloom in my time.
And when I'm ready,
I illuminate the garden
when she needs it
the most.

If you look for a pattern,
you will find it.
Choose your patterns wisely.

ENLIGHTENMENT

Like the trees
who sacrifice their leaves,
let me leave my regrets.
Let me leave my doubts.
Let me leave the thoughts
that stand in the way
of my self acceptance,
of my self love,
of my self.

A deliberate breath can be the thing that transforms the confines of a life into the freedom of living. I choose to breathe. I choose to live. I am no captive. I am free.

DON'T WAIT

Don't wait till it's over to breathe,
to let air expand your possibilities.
Don't wait till it's over to laugh,
to let joy elevate your vibration.
Don't wait till it's over to cry,
to let water clear your tension.
Don't wait till it's over to scream,
to let sound balance your system.
Don't wait till it's over to dance,
to let movement nurture your soul.
Don't wait till it's over to love,
to let spirit fulfill your manifestations.

HUNTER MOON AFFIRMATION

With a heart full of gratitude and joy, I personify the hunter moon, and I push. I reclaim my devotion and release my doubt. I invite hardship to transmute me, and I sacrifice only what no longer serves me. My chosen patterns are now my manifestation rituals. I know that in my life, I am always on time and divinely supported. Every breath I take is a confirmation: I commit to seeing my dreams through.

November Beaver Moon

COMPLETE

New Beaver Moon:
Reclaim Satisfaction

Full Beaver Moon: Release Attachment

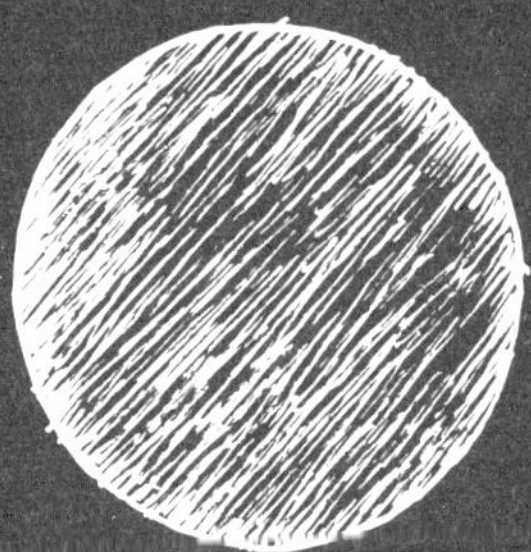

BEAVER MOON

November moon. Beaver moon.
Complete your mission moon.
Believe this is enough moon.
Let go of the rest moon.
Receive your fulfillment moon.
No time for self-judgment moon.
Choose to be finished moon.
Prepare to relax moon.
Satisfy yourself moon.
Be proud moon.

NOVEMBER MANIFESTATION

The end is here.
This year's work is complete.
Can you relinquish your attachments?
Will you allow yourself to rest?
Recognize how far you've come.
Stand tall in your reality.
Taste your satisfaction.
Reflect on your success.
You have arrived.
My love, you are here.

November is the time to make a "got it done" list instead of a "to do" list.

YOU ARE THE GARDENER

Yesterday's priorities are today's promise.
If you prioritized ease, you live an easy life.
If you prioritized play, you live a playful life.
If you prioritized love, you live a loving life.
If you prioritized your worth,
you live a worthwhile life.

A clonal tree colony, at first glance, appears to be made up of multiple individual trees. Yet beneath the surface, we discover that they share a vast, interconnected root system. Our manifestations work in the same way. Although they may seem separate on the surface, our grandest visions are often deeply connected. When we honor the fact that our dreams are part of something greater, we can complete our part in realizing them without being attached to finishing everything ourselves. We can surrender the ego's need for instant gratification and recognition and instead experience the profound satisfaction that comes with knowing we are sustained and carried forward by community.

Clonal tree colonies live longer and thrive better than independent trees. The same is true for us.

POMEGRANATES

I plant the seeds
for fruits I may never taste.
In seven years,
when the sweetness comes,
remember that today
I hoped its recipient
would be you.

You can know exactly how it will work out,
or you can experience the magic
of letting it unfold. I choose magic.

BLUE MOON

If a single month
can hold space for
not one but two full moons,
imagine the abundance
waiting for me
if I'm willing to look
beyond this year's
expected fullness.

Self love is saying no to the things
and people that don't work for you
anymore—even if you miss them.
It's also knowing when to say yes.

GOOD NATURE

My love language is
a good attitude.
Meet me with a smile,
right where we are.
Show me you are satisfied
and, lover, I am yours.

In November, the leaves fall, and the trees become bare. At first, we miss the lush greens of summer, the delicious fruit, the endless leaves and blooms. But it is only through November's nakedness that the fractal patterns within trees become truly visible. Fractals—repeating shapes and patterns that duplicate themselves as the tree grows from seed to sprout, twig to branch—demonstrate how small, consistent efforts can achieve something extraordinary. Without the shiny distractions, the strength of the tree's foundation becomes clear: every bit of the tree is imbued with its essence.

You've spent all year chasing your blooms, your goals. Now is the time to take it all in. Witness your own bare essence, marvel at your journey, and own every part of it.

LUNAR ALCHEMY

When the sun calls on you
to rise and become,
listen to the moon,
who reminds you that
waxing, waning, full, or new:
you already are.

When my daughter Violet was nine, she offered me this deep wisdom about trusting life to unfold without attachment: "Life is a puzzle. Every day, you find a new piece. One day, you will find all the pieces, and you will start a new puzzle."

This year's puzzle is coming to a close. Notice all the pieces you put in place. Recognize the pieces that just fell into place, too. It all came together, didn't it? As it usually does.

Now ask yourself: Can this year's work be enough?
Can you lovingly let this puzzle go?

MOON LOVERS, UNITE!

Let's blame it on the moon.
Together, let's be lunatics.
We gaze up in awe.
We fill up on wonder.
We trust the cycle.
We flow with the tides.
We dance beneath the stars.
We sleep among the flowers.
The moon made us do it.
We did it all with love.

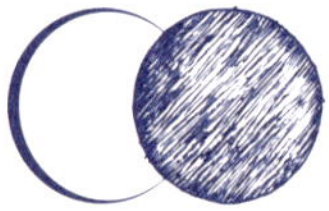

BEAVER MOON AFFIRMATION

With a heart full of gratitude and joy, I channel the beaver moon, and I complete my manifestations for the year. I reclaim my satisfaction and release my attachments. I take pride in my patterns and acknowledge the immense growth I've experienced. I gift myself time to nurture my long-term visions and invite my community to take part in realizing them. I root into love, again and again. I trust that for now, it is time to stop working, and I prepare to rest.

December Cold Moon

REST

New Cold Moon: Reclaim Peace

Full Cold Moon: Release Burdens

COLD MOON

December moon. Cold moon.
Enter your sanctuary moon.
Welcome the quiet moon.
Feel, don't do moon.
Listen to your body moon.
Turn off your mind moon.
Rest and be still moon.
Less is more moon.
Surrender your burdens moon.
Be at peace moon.

DECEMBER MANIFESTATION

You made it here.
You deserve this deep rest.
Can ease be your only aim?
What more can you put down?
Honor your softness.
Seek solace in the garden.
Spend more time with the moon.
End as you began.
Heart open yet again.

Letting go isn't losing.
Letting go is liberation.

FREEDOM

I held on
as long as I could
and when I let go
I realized I should
have done it sooner.

The sun accounts by days.
The moon accounts by months.
Follow the moon.
Give yourself time.

SUPERNOVA

You tried to break me
but didn't realize
stars don't succumb;
they become supernovas.
You tried to silence me
but didn't realize
moons don't disappear;
they rest and re-emerge.
You tried to control me
but didn't realize
universes don't shrink;
they expand infinitely,
new worlds born
after every heartbreak.

Forgive frequently, fully, and without hesitation. Forgive others. Forgive yourself. Forgive and quell the anger. Forgive and surrender the pain. Forgive and reclaim the space. Forgive and ease the burden. Forgive and heal your heart. Forgive and be at peace. Forgive. Forgive. Forgive. Now. Now. Now.

THE ONLY WORD SPOKEN IN THE GARDEN

Paz

Paix

Frieden

Pace

和平

平和

평화

صُلْح

शांति

Barış

Amani

Kedamaian

Vrede

Ειρήνη

שָׁלוֹם

Fred

Peace

After a lifetime spent racing toward milestones, resting can feel like something is wrong or missing. Part of deep healing is realizing that your life isn't a race to be won. In fact, life isn't quite as linear as we've been led to believe.

The finish line is a fallacy; the joy of being alive is never done.

WINTER SOULSTICE

In the wild night,
I'm carried by the wind
and held by the darkness.
There is no right direction,
no need to focus my gaze.
I gently linger; I softly notice.
I ease into the quiet cold.
In this beautiful unknown,
I am restored, I am rooted,
I receive a chorus of support.
The owls, the beetles,
the generous midnight moon,
they are all singing for me.

Learn from the bats that hibernate in the winter because they understand that sometimes, survival depends on slowing down and doing less. There will always be more work to do. You don't have to be done to earn the right to rest. And when you're ready, the garden is available.

THE GARDEN IS AVAILABLE

When you're tired,
the garden is available.
When you're burned out,
the garden is available.
When you've lost hope,
the garden is available.
When you've given up,
the garden is available.
The sanctuary you seek
is right outside your door.

I could write another poem about
what it means to be alive, but it's simpler
to send you out to the moon garden,
where you can find out for yourself.

HELLO, MOON

Goodnight, repression.
Goodnight, control.
Goodnight, resistance.
Goodnight, limitations.
Goodnight, isolation.
Goodnight, perfection.
Goodnight, fear.
Goodnight, shame.
Goodnight, disappointment.
Goodnight, doubt.
Goodnight, attachment.
Goodnight, burdens.

COLD MOON AFFIRMATION

With a heart full of gratitude and joy, I listen to the cold moon, and I rest. I reclaim my peace and release my burdens, leaving my struggles in the past. Time is my friend as long as I trust it. I cherish the manifestations that are already here, knowing that my deep rest sustains them. Whatever tomorrow brings, I know the moon will come along, too. In the garden, I am never alone. Under the light of the moon, I am at peace.

MOON GARDEN

poetry for manifestation

the garden

. . . is you

______________________ *AFFIRMATION*

YOUR NAME HERE

MELODY'S AFFIRMATION

With a heart full of gratitude and joy, I embody all the moons and manifest my dreams alongside kindred spirits around the world. My readers deeply enjoy Moon Garden: Poetry for Manifestation *and share it with their friends, family, and on social media using the hashtag #moongardenpoetry while tagging @melodygodfred and @moongardenpoetry. Readers joyfully go one step further and support me by rating and reviewing* Moon Garden *on Goodreads, Amazon, Barnes & Noble, and beyond. Each positive review makes it that much easier for someone new to join us on this collective manifestation journey as we bring our dreams—and each other's—to life.*

ACKNOWLEDGMENTS

Thank you, from the deepest parts of my moon-loving heart, to every reader who has read and shared my books so far. I love hearing from you and learning about how my work has made it easier for you to express, love, and honor your most authentic self.

I'm grateful to my mom for teaching me to love the moon, and to my dad for always bringing me back to the garden. Together, they have been, and always will be, my greatest inspiration and steadiest foundation.

Thank you to my partner in life, Aaron Godfred, who takes me out of my comfort zone and into nature. In my wedding vows, I quoted Rumi. Nearly fifteen years later, I continue to lovingly meet you in the field beyond the ideas of wrongdoing and rightdoing. May we never stop sealing our greatest wishes by looking up and saying, "By the moon!"

I'm also profoundly grateful to my children, Stella, Violet, and Teddy, who allowed me to share their stories here. They are my greatest teachers and the universe's clearest conduits. Thank you to my brother Jonny, who read many early drafts of these poems and lovingly gifted me with his gentle wisdom and healing presence. To Diana, my oldest and most cherished friend, your thoughtful feedback made this book better. And to Brady, who invited me to Ojai in June of 2023 and set this book into motion, and who recently taught me (after I finished this book) that "Ojai" means "moon" in Chumash (yet another divine affirmation), I am so thankful for you and our friendship.

My poetry career wouldn't be possible without my many champions at Andrews McMeel Publishing. From Patty Rice and Julie Barnes to Cat Vaughn and Danys Mares, every person at AMP has shown me nothing but the greatest love, enthusiasm, and care. Thank you for helping me connect with and honor my readers.

Finally, to every bookstore and bookseller that took a chance on me and stocked my books, I'll never stop being in awe that my books live in bookstores, my happy place since childhood. This is my greatest manifestation.

ABOUT THE AUTHOR

Melody Godfred is a poet, author, and speaker who is devoted to empowering people to love themselves and transform their lives. She is the creator of the Self Love Pinky Ring™ and author of Self Love Poetry: For Thinkers & Feelers; The ABCs of Self Love; The Shift: Poetry for a New Perspective; *and* Moon Garden: Poetry for Manifestation. *Her poetry has been recognized by* Oprah Daily, TODAY with Hoda & Jenna, *and Goodreads, among others, for its wisdom and ability to deeply resonate and uplift.*

Melody lives in Los Angeles with the loves of her life, Aaron, Stella, Violet, and Teddy. Learn more about booking Melody to speak at your next event at melodygodfred.com, connect with her on social media @melodygodfred, and join her newsletter at melodygodfred.substack.com.

Enjoy Moon Garden *as an audiobook narrated by the author, wherever audiobooks are sold.*